BRILLIANT BRITS
NELSON

RICHARD BRASSEY

Who had only one arm and a blind eye?

Who put his telescope to his blind eye and said he couldn't see anything?

Whose dead body was kept in a barrel of brandy for two months?

Whose statue stands on top of a tall column in the middle of London?

HORATIO NELSON

Horatio was born in 1758 in the small Norfolk village of Burnham Thorpe where his father was parson. His mother died when he was nine. She'd had eleven babies but only Horatio, two brothers and two sisters survived.

Burnham Thorpe is just two miles from the sea.

I never saw fear, Grandma. What is it?

Tell us about how you beat the French, uncle.

Although small for his age, Horatio was always very adventurous. Once he got lost in a wood all day. When his grandmother asked if he'd felt any fear, he replied that he didn't know what fear was. His Uncle Maurice was a captain in the Royal Navy. Horatio loved to listen to his stories.

When Horatio was only twelve, his uncle arranged for him to join his ship as a midshipman. These were boys who would one day become officers.

Midshipmen lived in a crowded cabin right at the bottom of the ship.

It was not as crowded as the gundeck above where several hundred ordinary seamen slept squashed together in hammocks. It must have been very smelly! Life in the Navy was so hard that there weren't enough volunteers. Ships often sent press-gangs ashore to kidnap men and force them to be sailors.

After a trip to the Caribbean, Horatio joined another ship, the *Carcass*, which was going to try and find a way around the North Pole to the Pacific. The *Carcass* got stuck in the ice. It was very cold. The sailors ate lots of pepper and mustard with every meal, which they thought would keep them warm.

During a fog, Horatio, now fifteen, sneaked off the ship to hunt a polar bear. The bear ended up hunting him instead. Only the ice cracking between them saved his life but he said later he hadn't been the least bit frightened.

Next Horatio sailed to India where he caught malaria. The voyage home was rough. He had a high fever and felt like throwing himself overboard until suddenly he saw a bright light and felt better. He decided then and there he would become a hero . . . at least that's the story he told later.

Horatio proved himself a good officer. He was made a captain aged only twenty-one and soon had a chance to become a hero by helping lead an expedition to capture a Spanish castle on the Mosquito Coast of Nicaragua. But he caught fever again and this time he nearly died.

When he eventually recovered, Horatio was given command of another ship in the Caribbean. He was always popular with his sailors. He never asked them to do anything he wouldn't do himself.

Hello, my name's Horatio. What's yours?

I order you up the mast-head. In fact I'll race you!

He got on well with children, too. While waiting to call on the President of the island of Nevis, he met a boy called Josiah under a table. Josiah's widowed mum, Fanny, was the President's niece. Horatio fell in love with her. They were married and returned to Burnham Thorpe. That winter was so cold, they spent most of it in bed.

BRRR! BRRR!

The war with France had ended and it was five frustrating years before Horatio went to sea again. After the French Revolution began and the French king and queen had had their heads chopped off, war broke out once more.

It's good to be back at sea again, Josiah.

Horatio was sent on a mission to ask for help from the King Ferdinand of Naples. Josiah, now 13, went with him as a midshipman. In Naples they stayed with the British ambassador, Sir William Hamilton, and his wife Emma.

I'm a little hurt . . . a very slight scratch.

The next few years were very eventful for Horatio.

On Corsica he was wounded and lost the sight in his right eye . . . OW!

At the battle of Cape St Vincent he rammed two Spanish ships and captured them both. His actions won the battle. He was made Sir Horatio. He also became an admiral.

Next he led an attack on the island of Tenerife but was shot in the right arm. The wound was so bad his arm had to be sawn off. There was no anaesthetic then ... OW! OW! OW!

I'm a dead man!

I hear you lost your right arm.

Only two days later he was busy writing letters with his left hand. When Fanny saw the strange handwriting, she wouldn't open her letter. She thought it must be to tell her he was dead.

Back in England, Horatio found he was a hero. He even met King George III.

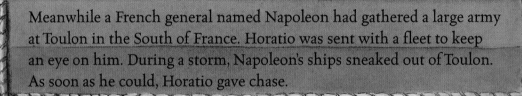

Meanwhile a French general named Napoleon had gathered a large army at Toulon in the South of France. Horatio was sent with a fleet to keep an eye on him. During a storm, Napoleon's ships sneaked out of Toulon. As soon as he could, Horatio gave chase.

TOULON

CORSICA
where Horatio lost the
sight in his right eye

ITALY

NAPLES
where Horatio
met Emma

Was Napoleon going to invade Naples? When Horatio got there everything was OK. He hurried on to Egypt. There was no sign there either. He raced back to Sicily, only to discover he must have overtaken Napoleon on the way to Egypt and passed him on the way back, missing him both times.

BRONTE
King Ferdinand made
Horatio Duke of
Bronte and gave him
a ruined castle here

SICILY

TO GIBRALTAR AND
THE ATLANTIC

MEDITERRANEAN
SEA

When news of the victory reached Naples, the city was lit up and everybody celebrated. Horatio had saved them from Napoleon and the French. He sailed into the bay a few days later to a hero's welcome.

Nelson rivals Caesar!

Emma held a birthday party for Horatio. She sang songs about him in a loud voice.

Oh, brave Nelson! Our saviour!

Mwaah!

Mwa

Emma has found the softest pillows for you.

I'm delirious with joy!

My head is splitting!

Horatio had a bad wound on his forehead. The Hamiltons made a big fuss and insisted he stay.

The Queen of Naples was sister of the Queen of France, who'd had her head chopped off. She fainted at the news. Then she kissed everybody.

Horatio stayed in Naples for nearly two years.
He and Emma began to fall in love even though
she was Sir William's wife.

When a French army invaded, Horatio helped
King Ferdinand and his queen escape to Sicily.

EMMA HAMILTON
wearing special Nelson earrings

Then he helped them win Naples back. He always thought
kings were wonderful even when perhaps they were not.
Ferdinand made him a duke and gave him loads of medals.

Meanwhile Napoleon had got back to France and made
himself ruler. When he invaded Italy yet again, Horatio
and the Hamiltons were ordered to return to England.

Horatio hadn't been home since the Battle of the Nile. He was the only man who had ever beaten Napoleon. Everybody wanted to honour him. Several pubs were renamed *The Nelson Arms* although, as he pointed out, he only had one.

When he called at the palace, George III was very put out by the title of duke and the sparkly medals that Ferdinand had given him . . . and the enormous wobbly diamond brooch in his hat. The Queen refused to meet him because he had split up with his wife and was having an affair with Emma.

People had thought it odd when Sir William married Emma, who was thirty years younger and a blacksmith's daughter. They thought it even odder when Horatio, Emma and Sir William spent Christmas 1800 together at Fonthill, the gigantic medieval-style home of William Beckford . . . but then he was odd too. After a feast of medieval food, which nobody much liked, Emma performed her famous *Attitudes*.

EMMA'S ATTITUDES
People marvelled as Emma, in flowing robes, took on the poses of ancient Greek and Roman statues. You have to remember there was no TV in those days.

FONTHILL ABBEY
25 years after the medieval feast the huge tower crashed down, destroying the house.

Happy Medieval Christmas!

Horatio was soon back at sea taking on the Danish fleet at Copenhagen. Old Admiral Parker watched from a safe distance. Thinking the battle was going badly, he signalled a retreat. Horatio put his telescope to his blind eye and claimed he couldn't see the signal. He went on to win the battle.

On his return Horatio was made a lord and put in charge of defending England. Everybody expected Napoleon to invade at any minute. But instead Napoleon signed a truce a few months later.

Horatio longed for a quiet family life. While he was away, Emma had had a baby girl. She named her Horatia because Horatio was her father. They found a country house near London where they could live together with Sir William.

PARADISE MERTON

But in those days a woman could not admit to having a baby with someone who wasn't her husband so little Horatia stayed with a lady in London. They visited her often.

If only Horatia were here this would be paradise!

THE NILE
They named the canal after Nelson's famous victory.

But after not much more than a year, Napoleon was planning invasion again. Horatio set to sea on HMS *Victory*, the finest ship in the Royal Navy. In his cabin he wrote endless letters to Emma and Horatia. He was so homesick.

When the French broke out of port, he chased them all the way to the Caribbean and then back to Spain. Here he left his ships and raced home to Merton. Horatia was now living there since old Sir William had died. It was the happiest month of his life.

Changing wet socks with one hand takes forever, so I walk about on the carpet to dry them.

EMMA

HORATIA

THE ADMIRAL'S CABIN

HMS VICTORY

THAT EVERY

DO   U   D

Number of trees to build: 6000
Miles of rope in the rigging: 26
Number of guns: 104
Number of men: 821
Youngest: Thomas Twitchet, 12

Then a message arrived. The French had broken out again. Sadly, he kissed Horatia goodbye as she slept. A large crowd cheered him off at Portsmouth. The sailors cheered even louder when he arrived back at the *Victory*.

The French fleet had joined the Spanish at Cadiz. On 20th October they came out of port. The next day Horatio ordered the flags on the *Victory* to signal: "England expects that every man will do his duty".

Horatio's friend, Captain Hardy, suggested he change his coat so his decorations didn't make him a target but Horatio was in a hurry.

It's too late to be shifting a coat.

THE BATTLE OF TRAFALGAR

The enemy were not expecting him to lead his ships straight into their guns. *Victory's* sails were shot to tatters but she smashed through their line, firing a broadside on the French admiral's ship. She turned at point blank range on another French ship. But the captain of *Le Redoubtable* had filled her rigging with musketeers. *Victory's* deck was a hail of bullets. All at once, Hardy turned and saw Horatio fall.

They have done for me at last, Hardy.

The surgeons below found a bullet hole in Horatio's shoulder. He was dying . . . The battle above raged on but the enemy had been broken. Hardy came down to tell him of their surrender. Horatio begged him to see that Emma and Horatia were taken care of. Then he asked him for a kiss. Hardy kissed him on the forehead.

A huge storm blew up, destroying many of the helpless enemy ships. Thousands were drowned. The wives of several sailors, who had disguised themselves as men, were among those rescued.

Little HMS *Pickle* took two weeks battling the waves to England with the news that Napoleon's navy had been destroyed . . . but Admiral Lord Nelson was dead.

The whole country came to a stop. The King was so upset he couldn't speak.

Horatio's body was put in a large cask of brandy to preserve it. A marine sentry guarded it day and night. Most of *Victory's* masts had been shot away. She had to be towed home.

After lying in state at Greenwich, a two-mile procession of boats escorted Horatio's coffin up the Thames to Whitehall. The procession behind his funeral car from Whitehall to St Paul's was so long that the front arrived before the end had started. Horatio had asked to be buried in St Paul's. He'd heard that Westminster Abbey was built on mud and would one day sink.

Feeling left out, the Abbey exhibited a life-size wax figure of Horatio. When Emma saw it, she burst into tears.

The papers published poems. Painters painted pictures. Countless souvenirs were made depicting him and his famous battles. Towns, streets, mountains and ships were named after him.

NELSON

Emma was heartbroken. In his will Horatio left her to the care of his country. But, because they were not married, the King ignored this. Emma soon spent the money Horatio had left her. She moved to France with Horatia and died in 1815.

Horatia returned to live with Horatio's sister. She married and lived happily to be eighty. She never knew Emma was her real mum. But she knew Horatio was her dad. Before Trafalgar, she'd asked him for a dog. He said he didn't have one on *Victory* but sent her a gold dog necklace instead. It was her most treasured possession.

Fanny lived until 1831. Josiah had been very angry when Horatio left his mother. He left the Navy and became quite rich in business.

Nelson's Column was completed forty years after Horatio's death. It stands in the middle of the London square named after his most famous battle. *Victory* was restored and you can visit her today in Portsmouth.